TOURIST RAILROADS OF NORTHERN CALIFORNIA

TOURIST RAILROADS OF NORTHERN CALIFORNIA

FOUR HISTORIC ATTRACTIONS OF THE GOLDEN STATE

MARK KLINGEL

AMERICA THROUGH TIME®
ADDING COLOR TO AMERICAN HISTORY

America Through Time is an imprint of Fonthill Media LLC
www.through-time.com
office@through-time.com

Published by Arcadia Publishing by arrangement with Fonthill Media LLC
For all general information, please contact Arcadia Publishing:
Telephone: 843-853-2070
Fax: 843-853-0044
E-mail: sales@arcadiapublishing.com
For customer service and orders:
Toll-Free 1-888-313-2665

www.arcadiapublishing.com

First published 2022

Typeset in 10pt on 13pt Sabon
Printed and bound in England

Contents

Introduction   7

1 The Niles Canyon Railway   9

2 Napa Valley Wine Train   31

3 The Sacramento Southern and the California State Railroad Museum   53

4 The Western Railway Museum   74

   Bibliography   96

Introduction

Since the middle of the 1800s, the state of California has become very well acquainted with the railroad industry thanks to the completion of the transcontinental railroad in 1869. As a direct result of the railroad industry's entrance, the economy boomed in ways it never had done so before and effectively changed the "Golden State" forever. As the years went by, the railroads would change themselves with the introduction of new technology and more modern pieces of equipment due to a continuous increase in demand for higher efficiency. One such method to increase efficiency and cut unnecessary costs was to shut down and abandon railroad lines that were no longer considered to be profitable—a practice that still continues to this day. The abandonment of these railroad lines helped give birth to a new tourist attraction: the tourist railroads.

Tourist railroads can be found in every corner of the globe. These typically small and scenic railroads are mostly operated by volunteers who devote their time to preserving railroad history and keeping it alive for generations to come, using railroad equipment that would normally be considered obsolete or outdated. However, there are some tourist railroads that are operated like a business. One such notable example is the Napa Valley Wine Train. Unlike the modern freight carriers that you see today, their sole commodity is the people that come to visit them and ride their trains. The people that visit these historic operations come from places near and far in order to get a glimpse of what railroading in the past was like or to experience the sights and scenery that are situated along their tracks.

California is littered with tourist railroads, some that are very well known and others not so much. In the northern end of California, there are four tourist lines and museums that are must visits for the average train enthusiast or for a family looking for something to do on a vacation or weekend. The Napa Valley Wine Train provides passengers with a unique experience of fine dining and wine tasting on their first-class passenger trains running past endless vineyards and wineries on a former Southern Pacific branch line. The Sacramento Southern, owned and operated by the California State Railroad Museum, offers their passengers a ride behind authentic locomotives through Old Town Sacramento and along the levees of the Sacramento River. The Western Railway Museum gives their passengers a taste of what electric railway transportation was like in the early twentieth century, using various trolleys, streetcars, interurban cars, and 22 miles of former Sacramento Northern and Union Pacific right of way. Utilizing a former Southern Pacific main line, the Niles Canyon Railway provides visitors a scenic ride through a high rising canyon behind classic steam and diesel locomotives between Sunol and Niles. Situated within a 100-mile radius of each other, these tourist railroads and museums contribute to their local economies as destinations and attractions for the general public.

1

The Niles Canyon Railway

Completed on May 10, 1869, at Promontory Point, Utah, the transcontinental railroad united the United States like never before. Contrary to popular belief, the world-famous rail line did not actually reach the West Coast upon its celebrated completion. At the time, the transcontinental railroad only stopped in Sacramento, California. The final rail link to the Pacific Ocean was not fully completed until four months after the Golden Spike Ceremony took place in Utah.

During those four months after the official celebration, track was being laid around the clock to truly unite the country from coast to coast. To reach the Pacific, workers began laying track out of Sacramento to Stockton. Before the celebrated completion, the first Western Pacific Railroad was formed in 1862 and the company constructed approximately 20 miles of track out of San Jose heading towards Sacramento. The Western Pacific reached into the canyon in 1866 and its first passenger trains began service on October 2, 1866.

Progress on any further construction was quickly brought to a halt when disagreements arose between the railroad's contractors and its financers. Sometime later, the Central Pacific Railroad acquired the Western Pacific as well as multiple other local railroads. The Central Pacific wasted no time in building track to connect them and finished the construction of the tracks through the canyon. By the autumn of 1869, this new addition to the transcontinental railroad would eventually reach its end on a ferry slip at Alameda Point on the San Francisco Bay.

The Central Pacific Railroad became part of the Southern Pacific Railroad Company in 1885. As the years passed on, Southern Pacific heavily invested in their main line north of Niles Canyon through Benicia and Martinez. As the main line to the north became more of a priority, the tracks in the canyon quickly assumed the role as a secondary main line. As a result of the lack of attention given to the canyon by the Southern Pacific, the Niles Canyon line still retains a majority of its original stone cut abutments, culverts, and retaining walls. Many of these features can still be seen today on various parts along the route of the Niles Canyon Railway whether you are driving along the highway that runs parallel to the tracks or taking a ride on the train between Sunol and Niles. The Southern Pacific Railroad continued main line operations in Niles Canyon until 1984, when it was decided to cease main line train operations entirely. The tracks were quickly pulled up and the land was deeded to Alameda County until 1987 when the Pacific Locomotive Association entered into an agreement with the county and set to work on rebuilding the line.

The Niles Canyon Railway currently operates approximately 9 miles of track between Niles Station and Verona Road east of Sunol. The tracks run through the canyon and along the cliffs with the Union Pacific's tracks and CA-84 (Niles Canyon Road) running parallel for most of the journey between Sunol and Niles. While the railroad does not have any active railroad signals in use to direct train traffic, multiple semaphore, searchlight, and wigwag crossing signals are located along the right of way. The wigwag crossing signals are actively used with a pair of crossings in Brightside while the remaining semaphore and searchlight signals stand along the right of way as display pieces.

The Pacific Locomotive Association operates and maintains a unique roster of steam and diesel locomotives. The active steam roster consists of Robert Dollar 2-6-2T no. 3, Quincy Railroad 2-6-2T no. 2, and Clover Valley Lumber 2-6-6-2T no. 4. Beginning in July 2019, the railway began operating recently restored Columbia River Belt Line Railway 2-4-4-2 no. 7, also known as *"Skookum"*, on excursion trains under a lease agreement with the Oregon Coast Scenic Railroad. As of March 2020, the Pacific Locomotive Association has begun the operational restoration of Southern Pacific 2-6-0 Mogul no. 1744. The diesel locomotives of Niles Canyon handle the excursion trains during the middle of the summer months to minimize the risk of a fire breaking out during fire season. Many of these classic diesels are dressed in their original Southern Pacific and Western Pacific colors.

Southern Pacific NW-2 diesel switcher No. 1423 and the Niles Canyon excursion train arrive at Sunol Station after a routine excursion trip to Niles, CA.

Once the excursion train arrives in Niles, the locomotive is run around the train using the station siding in Niles. The crew operating Southern Pacific 1423 is seen here performing the routine run-around manoeuvre.

Left: Southern Pacific GP-9 No. 5623 crosses over Niles Canyon Road and Alameda Creek in Dresser. No. 5623 sports the Southern Pacific's *Black Widow* paint scheme that was commonly seen on Southern Pacific diesel locomotives from the 1940s to the early 1970s.

Below: Rounding the curve at Brightside, Southern Pacific 5623 leads its excursion train eastbound back to Sunol, CA. The crew on board slows the train down as it begins to approach the Niles Canyon Railway's yard limits.

While most of the signals along the right of way in Niles Canyon are now gone, a few deactivated signals still remain as display pieces. Among the small collection of signals in Niles Canyon, this searchlight signal in Farwell is the last of its kind still standing along the right of way between Sunol and Niles. Outside of Niles Canyon, searchlight signals can still be found in service on numerous railroads across the country.

Wigwag railroad crossing signals were once very common at most street and grade crossings across North America until modern electronic flashing signals replaced them. These signals are now are a rarity to find outside of a museum or tourist railroad as the revenue freight railroads of today quickly replaced wigwags with the electronic flashing signals you see at a modern-day railroad crossing.

Heading westbound with an excursion, Southern Pacific 1423 slows the train down to a safer speed as the train approaches the Brightside yard limits on the east end of the line.

Having cleared the yard in Brightside, 1423 throttles up once again as the westbound excursion train proceeds to head deeper into Niles Canyon.

Above: Southern Pacific SW9 No. 1195 and Western Pacific GP-7 No. 713 sit outside of the shops in Brightside waiting for their next assignment.

Right: No. 1423 passes by one of the deactivated Southern Pacific semaphore signals while on its way back to Sunol.

Left: Semaphore signals, like the wigwag crossing signals, were once a common sight on railroads throughout North America. Semaphore signals had their earliest beginnings in the 1840s and were, over time, replaced by modern-day color light signals. Mechanical signals like the semaphore have almost completely disappeared from the North American railroad main line and are now mostly present in museums or tourist railroads like Niles Canyon. Being a former Southern Pacific main line, these signals represent an era that has long since ended.

Below: Various pieces of railroad equipment in storage in Niles Canyon's Brightside yard.

A young couple watches 5623 run around its train in Sunol for its next excursion to Niles.

No. 5623 arrives back at Sunol Station, wrapping up a day of diesel-powered excursions in the canyon.

Heading westbound in Dresser, *Skookum* crosses one of two steel bridges crossing over Niles Canyon Road and Alameda Creek.

No. 5623 crosses over the steel bridge in Farwell.

Above: A family watches *Skookum* run around its train using the siding in Sunol.

Right: A view of the Drewer Bridge from on board the excursion train in Dresser.

Southern Pacific 1423 rolls across the bridge in Farwell spanning over Niles Canyon Road and Alameda Creek. No. 1423 wears the "Tiger Stripe" scheme that was applied to many SP diesel switchers between 1947 and 1958, prototypical to when it was built for Southern Pacific in 1949.

A view of the steel bridge in Farwell from on board the excursion train.

Skookum leads its excursion eastbound to Sunol in Farwell.

As *Skookum* rounds the bend in Farwell running tender first, a young boy and his grandfather ride on top of the tender. The engineer blows the whistle for the Farwell Bridge ahead of them, causing the young boy to cover his ears from the sudden wailing whistle of the old steam locomotive.

Left: A line of disused freight cars sit on a small siding in storage at the east end of Farwell.

Below: Skookum rounds the bend at Farwell before leading its train across the Farwell Bridge.

Above: Having cleared the Brightside yard limits, 5623 proceeds east on the final leg of the journey back to Sunol.

Right: After clearing the Brightside yard limits, the engineer opens up the throttle as *Skookum* picks up speed on the home stretch to Sunol.

A Santa Fe steel caboose sits in storage in Brightside yard.

Skookum crossing the steel bridge in Farwell.

Columbia River Belt Line 2-4-4-2 Mallet *Skookum* at Brightside.

Skookum arriving at Sunol Station.

Skookum approaching the station in Niles, CA, with a westbound excursion train.

Columbia River Belt Like Railway No. 7, named *Skookum*, is a 2-4-4-2 Mallet-type steam locomotive built by the Baldwin Locomotive Works in 1909. Locomotives like *Skookum* were designed to be light enough in terms of weight to operate on flimsy tracks of logging railroads and be powerful enough to exceed the pulling capacity of conventional steam locomotives of the time. *Skookum* is a Native American name meaning "powerful, brave, sturdy, tough, durable, and exceptional."

Right: Skookum splits the old SP semaphore signals standing just beyond the station in Sunol.

Below: SP 1423 approaching Niles, CA, at Vallejo Mill.

Southern Pacific 5623 looks right at home operating on former SP right of way while splitting old SP semaphore signals.

No. 5623 idling at Sunol Depot as passengers prepare to disembark.

No. 5623 arrives at Sunol Depot with its regular excursion train.

No. 5623 crosses the grade crossing at Brightside before entering the Niles Canyon Railway's main yard.

Skookum clears the yard limits at Brightside.

2

Napa Valley Wine Train

California's Napa Valley is known worldwide for three things: the gorgeous scenery, the wine train that traverses the world-famous wine country daily, and—most importantly—the wine. Traveling between Napa and St. Helena, California, the Napa Valley Wine Train offers passengers a luxurious train ride through the valley's seemingly endless vineyards and wineries that line the tracks and the highway running between the two cities. The Wine Train offers a number of unique experiences on board their trains, giving their passengers lots of options to choose from. These experiences include: the Gourmet Express, the Legacy Tour, Grgich Hills Winery Tour, Romance on the Rails, Murder Mystery, and many more. Some of these trains mentioned make stops at the local wineries situated along the right of way so that passengers may partake in wine tasting as well as take a tour of the facilities.

The line the Napa Valley Wine Train regularly travels on was built in 1864 by San Francisco millionaire Samuel Brannan to transport visitors to and from his luxury spa resort in Calistoga, California. The overall success of his railroad and resort venture would quickly come to an end when Brannan was forced to sell off a significant majority of his holdings to pay for a divorce. As a result of the divorce, the railroad line became the property of the California Pacific Railroad. About twenty years later in 1885, the Southern Pacific Railroad bought the Napa Valley Railroad.

From 1885 up until the 1930s, the Napa Valley line became a critical part of the economic development of the area by providing freight and passenger service to the local communities. Services under the Southern Pacific began to decline in the 1930s with the introduction of the automobile. The people of the Napa Valley quickly took to the roads which resulted in passenger service being discontinued indefinitely. By 1960, the railroad was having a difficult time keeping the branch line profitable. That same year, Southern Pacific abandoned the right of way between St. Helena and Calistoga and cut down train traffic on the branch to one freight train a week on the remaining tracks.

In a last-ditch effort to make some form of profit on the dying branch line, Southern Pacific made the final decision to abandon the line and sell the property in 1984. Word quickly spread about the abandonment of the branch line throughout the valley, and a group of residents did not want to see the historic railroad line go. After discovering the Southern Pacific's plans to abandon the line, retired Southern Pacific engineer Lou Schuyler formed "The Society for the Preservation of the Napa Valley Railroad." Schuyler and the newly formed society wasted no time in placing a rail-saving measure on the Napa County ballot. Unfortunately for them, the initiative failed to pass. However, the very high amount of support from the public caught the interest of a group of Napa citizens.

This new group, with the goal to preserve the railroad and reduce congestion on Napa Valley's roads, became known as the Napa Valley Wine Train Inc. and was founded by Dr. Alvin Lee Block. The Napa Valley Wine Train began the task of finding investors in 1987. Their search would eventually lead them to Vincent DeDomenico, who made his fortune through being the inventor of Rice-A-Roni as well as being the former owner of Ghirardelli Chocolate and Golden Grain Pasta. He ended up liking the idea of the Wine Train and made an offer to buy the entire operation, which resulted in him gaining a majority of the company's shares as well as being appointed as the president and CEO.

Thanks to his newly gained involvement, Napa Valley Wine Train was financially able to buy the branch line from the Southern Pacific. The company then set to work purchasing and restoring numerous pieces of antique locomotives and rolling stock, many of which are still in service today. On September 16, 1989, the Napa Valley Wine Train made its first run and has become a mainstay attraction in the world-famous wine country.

The trains originate out of Napa and run north towards St. Helena while passing through the neighboring communities of Yountville, Oakville, and Rutherford. Depending on the length and type of experience passengers are riding the train for, the locomotive(s) run around their train in one of the many sidings situated along the line before bringing the train back south to Napa. The railroad's roster consists of a fleet of diesel locomotives from the 1940s and 1960s. The railroad currently operates: GE-65 ton switcher no. 52, GE-80 ton switcher no. 57, ALCO RS-11 no. 62, and EMD GP9R no. 69. The railroad also operates a former Norfolk Southern high hood GP38-2 no. 5076 on a lease agreement from an outside owner. Napa Valley Wine Train also keeps a small roster of ALCO FPA-4s—nos. 70–73—which are all currently out of service awaiting a final decision from management regarding their future on the Napa Valley roster.

Right: Napa Valley GP38-2 No. 5076 rounds the bend with the northbound lunch train bound for St. Helena, CA.

Below: The Napa Valley Wine Train's main line is situated next to dozens of vineyards and wineries between Napa and St. Helena, CA. Napa Valley's GE 80-ton diesel switcher No. 57 leads the "Legacy Tour" excursion out of St. Helena while passing Sutter Home Winery and Louis M. Martini Winery.

A lone reefer sits on a siding as an art display piece in Napa, CA. This reefer is one of many various pieces of freight railroad equipment that are scattered on many small sidings located along the Napa Valley right of way.

As No. 57 brings the Legacy Tour train out of the yard to start the day, a group of retired ALCO FPAs sit in the deadline siding awaiting a decision on their future. Strict emission standards have quickly made these old streamlined diesel locomotives obsolete.

Napa Valley No. 57 leads the excursion train south back to Napa in Yountville, CA.

GP38-2 No. 5076 leads one of Napa Valley's first excursion trains since closing their doors due to the COVID-19 pandemic. Upon re-opening, the Legacy Tour would remain as the only operating excursion train on the Napa Valley line until a few weeks later when it was decided that the lunch and dinner train excursions would resume service in June.

Above: Heading southbound with the Lunch Train excursion, 5076 makes a quick stop at Grgich Hills Estate to drop off passengers.

Left: After a long day of winery tours, Napa Valley No. 57 brings the Legacy Tour back into urban Napa, CA.

Napa Valley No. 57 and the Legacy Tour depart St. Helena. The train passes by Louis M. Martini Winery before making the trains next scheduled stop at V. Sattui Winery.

No. 5076 leads the impressive Napa Valley Lunch and Dinner train southbound back to Napa. No. 5076 is a former Norfolk Southern high-hood GP38-2 that is operating in Napa Valley under a lease agreement until Napa Valley Wine Train makes more suitable upgrades to their locomotive roster.

The Napa Valley welcome sign is a local landmark that is a popular spot for tourists to take photos. While a large group of people are occupied with taking pictures in front of a sign, a small family watches 5076 and the Lunch Train pass by.

A local elderly citizen waves to the crew and passengers on board the Napa Valley Lunch Train excursion.

Above: A group of tourists pose for a photo in front of the Napa Valley welcome sign while the Legacy Tour excursion makes a scheduled stop. Bringing up the rear of the train, the open-air car *Mariposa* is fitted with a wine-tasting bar for passengers to drink wine on board the train while taking in the scenic views of Napa Valley's wine country.

Right: Open-air car *Mariposa* brings up the rear of the Legacy Tour as the train slows down for a scheduled stop at the Napa Valley welcome sign.

Napa Valley No. 57 leads the Legacy Tour out of St. Helena. As shown here, No. 57 still sports its U.S. Army paint scheme.

Napa Valley No. 57 and the Legacy Tour pass by the colorful reefer in Napa, CA.

Running long hood forward, Napa Valley GP9R No. 69 and the Legacy Tour pass by an old boxcar before entering Napa's city limits. No. 69 is a former Portland & Western Railroad locomotive that entered service on the Napa Valley in 2016.

Napa Valley ALCO RS-11 No. 62 sits outside of the Napa Valley Wine Train's shops alongside 80-ton switcher No. 57 and 65-ton switcher No. 52. Off to the side in the deadline, Napa Valley's ALCO FPAs sit silently in storage.

A pair of local elderly men wave to the engineer as the Legacy Tour passes by North Pole Station.

Napa Valley Railroad railway post office car sitting in a siding on static display in Rutherford, CA.

No. 5076 leads its northbound excursion train past Oakville Grocery in Oakville, CA.

No. 5076 heads southbound past one of the many vineyards that call Napa Valley home.

No. 5076 and the Legacy Tour excursion pass by GP9R No. 69 at the junction in Rutherford.

No. 5076 and the southbound Lunch Train excursion pass by the Provenance Vineyards.

Following the Lunch Train south back to Napa, the Legacy Tour rolls by Provenance Vineyards shortly after departing V. Sattui Winery.

A pair of bicyclists wave to the passengers riding on the Legacy Tour excursion train.

Above: Napa Valley's trio of retired FPAs sitting silently in the deadline.

Left: The Legacy Tour train passing by Robert Mondavi Winery southbound.

No. 5076 leads the northbound Lunch Train excursion through Rutherford Junction.

No. 5076 leads one of the first Legacy Tour excursions of the year past Sutter Home Winery.

Open-air *Mariposa* on the Legacy Tour excursion train.

No. 5076 passing by Sutter Home Winery northbound.

Napa Valley GP9R No. 69 throttles up with a southbound Legacy Tour excursion in Zinfadel.

Napa Valley No. 57 passing by a local winery.

The Legacy Tour approaches Dwyer Road crossing northbound.

V. Sattui Winery is the last scheduled stop for the Legacy Tour excursion. Once passengers board the train after a tour of the winery and some wine tasting, the excursion will highball southbound back to Napa, CA.

The Legacy Tour arrives at V. Sattui Winery for the last winery tour of the day.

Napa Valley No. 57 and the Legacy Tour rounding the bend in Yountville.

No. 5076 and the Legacy Tour excursion train wait for the day's passengers to finish their tour of V. Sattui Winery.

3

The Sacramento Southern and the California State Railroad Museum

Located in Old Town Sacramento Historic Park in Sacramento, California, the California State Railroad Museum has established itself as a must visit destination for anyone looking for places to visit while visiting one of California's largest cities. The museum boasts a large collection of historic steam and diesel locomotives with some of their oldest steam locomotives dating back to early 1860s. While a majority of their collection are on static display, some of their locomotives have been restored to operational condition in order to operate the excursion train rides on the Sacramento Southern Railroad. Some of their more well-known pieces of equipment include: Southern Pacific E9A no. 6051, Santa Fe F7 no. 347C, Southern Pacific 4-2-4T no. 1 *C.P. Huntington*, Granite Rock 0-6-0T no. 10, Western Pacific F7 no. 913, Virginia & Truckee 2-4-0 no. 21 *J.W. Bowker*, Union Pacific 0-6-0 no. 4466, and Southern Pacific 4-8-8-2 Cabforward no. 4294. While the full-sized train exhibits remain mostly on the first floor of the museum, the second and third floors house a large model train exhibit as well as other interactive exhibits that museum guests can visit.

The tracks of the Sacramento Southern begin in Old Town Sacramento at the Central Pacific Freight Depot and continue for another 3 miles along the Sacramento River. Departing from the freight depot, the excursion train takes its passengers south along the Sacramento River levees. After departing Old Town and crossing CA-275, the train slowly winds its way towards Front Street, where the train does a small amount of street running along a paved alleyway running parallel to Front Street. The line continues to follow Front Street to Pioneer Landing Park, where the rails and the road split off from each other. The tracks, as well as the bike trail that runs parallel to them, hug the shoreline of the Sacramento River for the whole journey through urban Sacramento. Once the train reaches a small junction located next to Interstate 5, the locomotive is then run around the train and proceeds back north along the river to Old Town Sacramento. Having had more than 1 million guests climb aboard for a ride along the Sacramento River, the excursion trains of the Sacramento Southern have been a mainstay attraction in Sacramento since 1982.

The original Sacramento Southern Railroad was a non-operating subsidiary company of the Southern Pacific that was incorporated in 1903. The railroad was built and operated on approximately 31 miles of track, running deep into the delta's rich agricultural area. The line was first constructed between 1906 and 1912 and was extended to Isleton in 1929 and later the Mokelumne River in 1931. The first trains began operating over the line in 1909, and the railroad merged with the Central Pacific in 1912. The railroad soon became known as the Walnut Grove Branch and served the communities of Freeport, Hood, Locke, Walnut Grove, and Isleton by hauling the many agricultural products that they produced. The railroad officially became part of the Southern Pacific in October 1978, when the Southern Pacific decided to abandon the line due to the increase in competition from trucks as well as flood damage to the right of way.

Heading south with a full train of passengers, Sacramento Southern SW8 No. 2008 leads the weekend excursion train across the crossing at Broadway Street before entering Miller Regional Park.

After clearing the Sacramento Southern's yard limits at the edge of Old Town Sacramento, SW8's 2008 and 2030 ease their excursion train southbound along Front Street. While 2030 sports the official Sacramento Southern gray paint scheme, 2008 still sports its former U.S. Army colors.

Street running has become a rare sight in the twenty-first century. The Sacramento Southern's main line keeps a part of that history alive with their tracks running down the center of an old side street at the south end of Old Town Sacramento.

SSRR 2030 shoves the excursion out of the railroad's Central Pacific Depot on a routine passenger trip along the Sacramento River.

SSRR 2030 leads its excursion train through the curve at Broadway Street before entering Miller Regional Park.

Diesel switchers like 2030 spent a majority of their time marshalling freight and passenger cars around railroad yards and terminals large and small alike. While 2030 waits to depart with another weekend excursion at Central Pacific Depot, Santa Fe 4-8-4 Northern No. 2925 sits on static display in a neighboring siding.

SSRR 2030 eases its way along Front Street with a matching passenger consist in tow.

Southern Pacific 4-6-2 Pacific No. 2467 sits on static display inside the museum's storage and display barn.

As shown here with SSRR 2030, a street-running train is a train that runs on railroad track that is routed directly on public streets. Street running was very common back in the nineteenth and twentieth centuries in many towns and cities. As the years progressed into the late twentieth century and early twenty-first century, street-running trains have gradually become a rare sight to see.

Santa Fe 347C is an F7A diesel locomotive that was built in 1949 by GM-EMD for the Atchison, Topeka & Santa Fe Railroad. Diesel locomotives such as 347C quickly replaced steam locomotives such as Santa Fe 4-8-4 Northern 2925 and Santa Fe 2-10-4 Texas 5021 in the 1950s and 1960s. After spending several years working for the Santa Fe, 347C was donated to the California State Railroad Museum in 1986 in its original Santa Fe "war-bonnet" colors. Today, 347C is put on static display in operable condition and is sometimes operated for special occasions.

Santa Fe 2925 on display in one of the sidings situated next to Central Pacific Depot.

Santa Fe 2-10-4 5021 sitting on display in one of the sidings next to Central Pacific Depot.

SSRR 2008 leads the excursion train southbound across Capital Mall Road with Sacramento's Tower Bridge standing tall and proud.

As SSRR 2008 waits to depart for its next excursion along the levees of the Sacramento River, Southern Pacific DRS66-1500 switcher No. 5208 sits on display in a siding with an SP Daylight passenger coach.

CSRM's 25-ton switcher No. 2 towing ATSF 347C in a storage rotation move.

Sacramento Southern observation car *El Dorado*.

Central Pacific Railroad 4-4-0 American *Gov. Stanford* on indoor display at the California State Railroad Museum.

CSRM's No. 2 waits to head out onto the main line with Santa Fe 347C for the storage move off of the museum grounds.

Virginia & Truckee Railroad 2-4-0 *J. W. Bowker* on display inside the California State Railroad Museum.

SSRR 2030 leads the excursion train back north through Miller Park on its way back to Old Town Sacramento.

SSRR 2008 and 2030 shove the excursion train back to Central Pacific Depot in Old Town Sacramento.

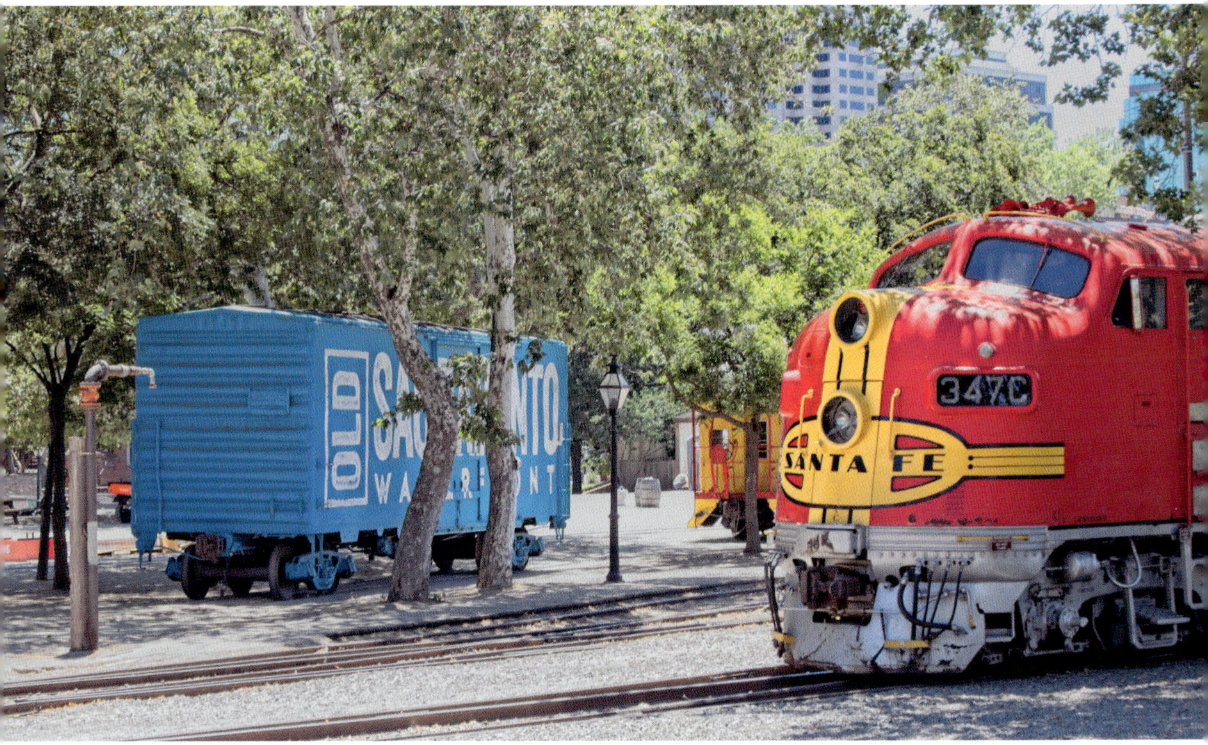
OLD
347C
SANTA FE

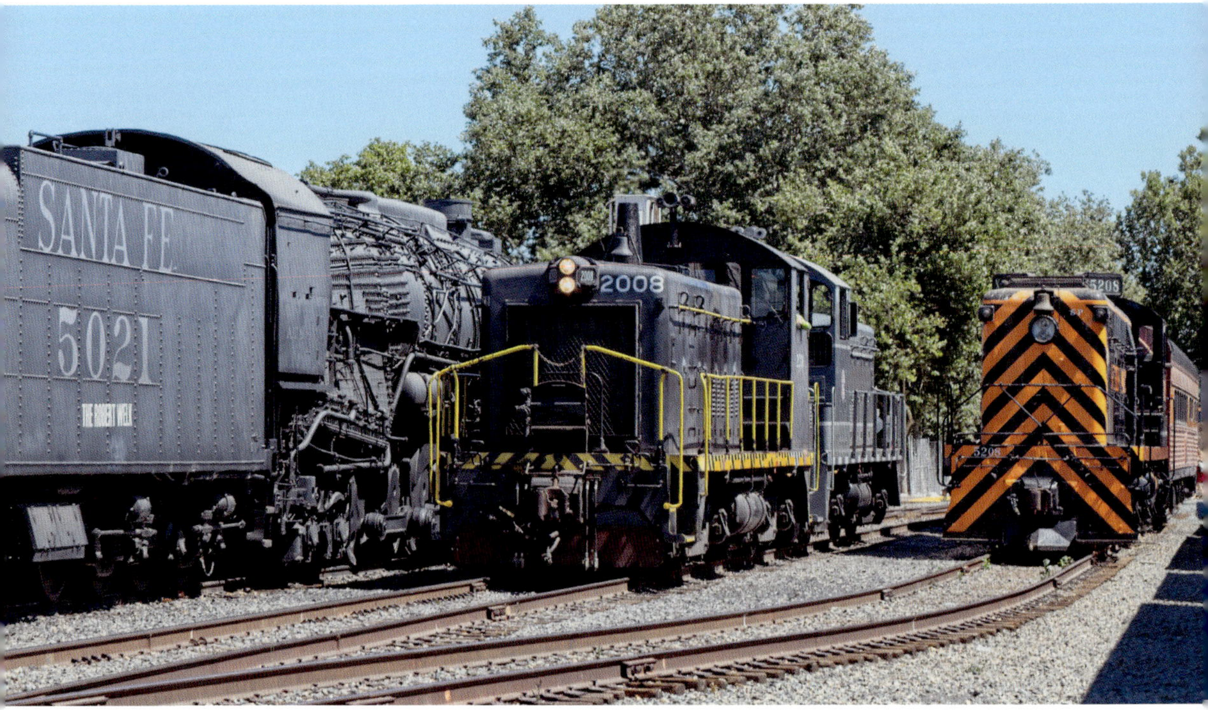
SANTA FE
5021
2008
5208

SSRR 2030 and 2008 lead the excursion train back to Old Town Sacramento with a Southern Pacific Daylight passenger coach in tow.

Opposite above: Santa Fe 347C basks in the sun next to the Old Sacramento Waterfront boxcar while waiting to be moved into storage.

Opposite below: SW8's 2008 and 2030 run around their train, while Southern Pacific 5208 and Santa Fe 5021 bask in the sun while on outdoor display.

Southern Pacific DRS66-1500 switcher No. 5208 sits on display with a daylight coach coupled up behind it. No. 5208 was donated to the museum in 1978 and was restored to its 1949 appearance in 1988.

Southern Pacific E9A 6051 backs out of the CSRM storage and display barn before taking a spin on the turntable. No. 6051 proudly sports its original SP Daylight colors and is occasionally used for special occasions.

Steam locomotives like Southern Pacific 4294 are known as the "Cabforwards" and were frequently used on heavy freight trains going over Southern Pacific's famous Donner Pass. The large number of tunnels and snow sheds that populated the Donner Pass route made it hard for train crews to breathe inside when operating conventional steam locomotives that constantly produced large amounts of smoke. Locomotives such as 4294 helped crews see and breathe better when operating freight and passenger trains in the mountains. Among the hundreds of Cabforwards built for the Southern Pacific Railroad, 4294 is now the only surviving example of its kind.

Opposite above: Southern Pacific Cabforward No. 4294's tender on display inside of the California State Railroad Museum.

Opposite below: SSRR 2008 slowly heads south out of Old Town Sacramento with another excursion. The train slowly winds its way between the many old-style buildings that occupy Old Town.

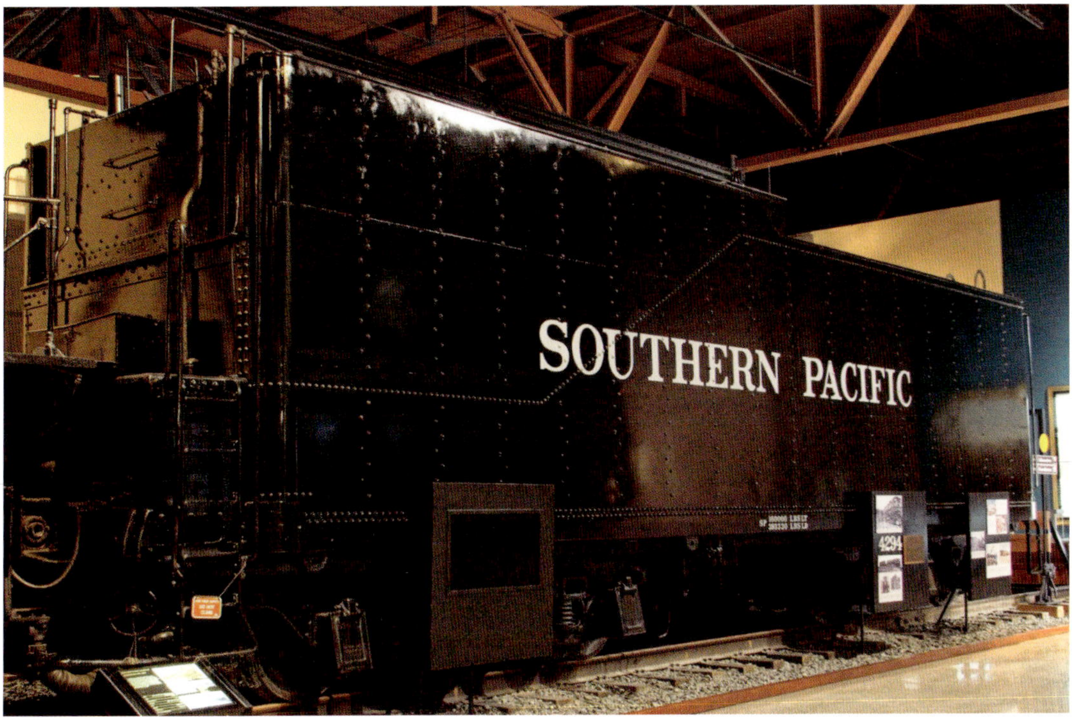
SOUTHERN PACIFIC
4294

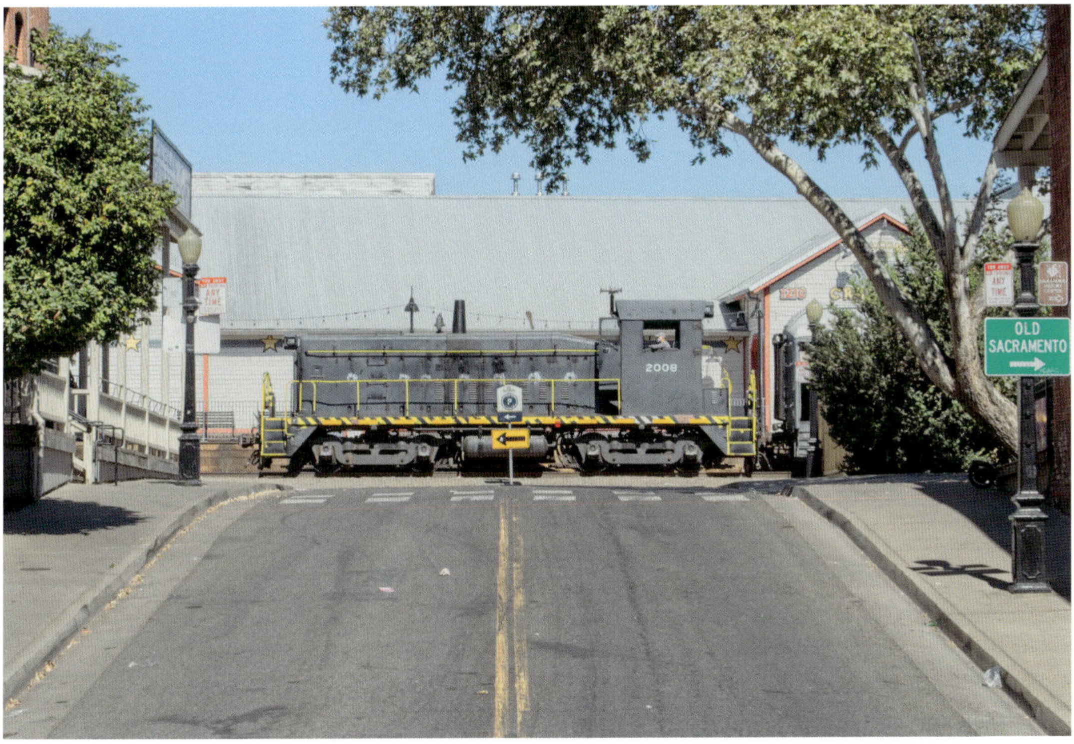
2008
OLD
SACRAMENTO

Having to run around their train at Central Pacific Depot, 2008 and 2030 meet CSRM No. 2 and Santa Fe 347C nose-to-nose in order for the two larger diesel switchers to clear the switch. No. 2 is waiting for the excursion train to depart Old Town so that it can position the Santa Fe diesel veteran behind it for a storage move.

A Union Pacific Railroad caboose sits on outdoor static display in front of Central Pacific Depot.

Virginia and Truckee Railroad 2-6-0 *Empire* sits on static display inside of the California State Railroad Museum.

Santa Fe 5021 and SP 5208 on display in Old Town Sacramento.

4

The Western Railway Museum

In the early years of the twentieth century, the age of steam was still going strong and the diesel locomotive concept was still in its earliest stages of development. While steam dominated on the main line, locomotives powered by electricity gained momentum in the more urban areas of North America. The railroads that operated these locomotives became known as interurbans or traction railroads. The interurban was a type of electric railway with streetcar-like self-propelled rail cars that ran within and between cities as well as surrounding towns. Interurbans and their suburban counterparts, the streetcars, were once common throughout the country between 1900 and 1925. The interurban and traction railroads of America would meet their end by World War II with only a small handful of them surviving into the 1950s. Most of these interurban lines either went out of business or became short line freight carriers in order to survive. One former interurban railroad that is still in business today using original electric traction locomotives is the Iowa Traction Railway.

The Western Railway Museum is located in Suisun City, California, and has become a haven for interurbans, trolleys, streetcars, and electric railroad equipment. While the name "Western Railway Museum" was not adopted until 1985, the museum's beginnings date back to 1946 when a group of people who chartered an Oakland streetcar discovered that it was scheduled to be retired and scrapped within the week. Not wanting to see the old streetcar meet the scrapper's torch, the members of the group pitched in money to buy the streetcar on the spot. After the purchase of the streetcar, the Bay Area Electric Railroad Association was born. Following the purchase of their first streetcar, the Bay Area Electric Railroad Association would spend the next several years acquiring a number of interurbans and streetcars to add to their growing collection. By the 1960s, the rapidly growing size of their collection would eventually result in the collection being moved to the 22 acres of vacant property next to the Sacramento Northern main line that the Western Railway Museum still resides on today.

The Western Railway Museum acquired the last remaining 22 miles of track that ran by their property in 1993 when the Union Pacific Railroad sold the remaining Sacramento Northern tracks to the museum. Since acquiring the former Sacramento Northern main line, volunteers at the museum have worked to rehabilitate the line to operate their interurban and streetcar roster. Volunteers have to slowly re-electrify their main line due to the Sacramento Northern ending their electric operations in 1965, which resulted in the overhead wires being permanently removed. The museum has currently electrified 5 miles of track between the museum and Birds Landing, which has allowed the museum to give their passengers a 10-mile round trip excursion on their Interurban train rides.

The Interurban excursion departs from the main station platform next to Car House Number One and works its way off the property to head south on the main line towards Birds Landing. Once on the main line, the train rolls southbound past the local wind farm, which can be seen between Little Honker Bay Road and Shiloh Road. Before reaching Shiloh Road, the train passes by the historic Shiloh Church and Gum Grove. During the fall season, the trains make station stops at Gum Grove for the museum's pumpkin festival. After passing through Gum Grove, the train crosses Shiloh Road and continues to roll south through the countryside towards Pantano and Birds Landing. The train stops for a brief layover in Pantano before reversing the train north to the museum. The museum also operates a shorter streetcar ride around the museum property. Using one of the various streetcars the museum owns, visitors are shown what riding in a streetcar would have been like in the early twentieth century. The train leaves the main platform next to car house number one and makes a brief stop at the Laflin Park station shack before proceeding south towards the main junction leading to the old Sacramento Northern main line the museum uses for the Interurban trips. Once at the edge of the 22-acre property line, the streetcar then reverses back north to the main station platform.

Today, the museum maintains and operates a wide variety of interurban and streetcar equipment from numerous interurban railroads that were scattered throughout North America. Such examples include: The Key System, Sacramento Northern Railroad, Pacific Electric Railroad, Petaluma & Santa Rosa, Oregon Electric, Cedar Rapids & Iowa City, San Francisco Municipal Railway, Pacific Gas & Electric, and San Francisco & Napa Valley. The museum also owns a pair of steam locomotives: Western Pacific 4-6-0 no. 94 (on static display in the Loring Jensen Memorial Car House) and Western Pacific 2-8-2 no. 334 (in indoor storage). With a unique assortment of railroad equipment on display, the museum gives visitors the unique experience of reliving the days of the interurban before its quick demise in the 1940s.

Key System No. 187 and East Bay Street Railway No. 352 wait at the museum's station platform for passengers.

The museum's Interurban ride takes passengers deep into the hot and dry California countryside. The ride stops at the current turnaround point at Pantano. The museum is currently in the process of restoring track south of Pantano at Birds Landing.

Making another trip around the museum's grounds on the streetcar ride, East Bay Street Railway No. 352 passes by the old Laflin Park station hut.

Sacramento Northern steeple cab unit No. 654 backs into the museum's Loring Jensen Memorial Car House while Key System No. 1201 sits on temporary outdoor display.

Electric-powered locomotives like 654 were used primarily in freight service for small interurban railroads like the Sacramento Northern. No. 654's career on the Sacramento Northern would end in 1965 when the railroad decided to cease electric operations entirely.

San Francisco Municipal Railway No. 1016 moves out of the memorial car house in preparation for the day's activities.

Portland Traction Company No. 4001 takes passengers past the wind turbines overlooking the crossing at Garfield.

No. 4001 begins the return journey back to the museum as it approaches Gum Grove station.

No. 4001 crosses the small trestle at Gum Grove.

No. 4001 slowly glides by the Gum Grove station platform on its way to Pantano. Gum Grove is a station stop primarily used for the museum's fall season events and festivities.

Interior of Portland Traction Company No. 4001.

Operating as the streetcar ride around the museum grounds, 4001 makes a brief simulated station stop at Laflin Park.

Overhead electric wires are the primary source of power for interurban cars and streetcars of the early twentieth century.

Interurban cars like Key System 187 were built with an articulated design and typically ran in trains of up to seven units. No. 187 and her sisters provided passenger service across the Bay Bridge and in the East Bay streets from 1939 until 1958.

Key System 187 approaches Gum Grove on the return journey back to the museum.

A maintenance of way vehicle follows Key System 187 back to the museum after concluding a day of track work at Birds Landing.

Key System 187 slowly glides past the station platform at Gum Grove.

Melbourne & Metropolitan Tram Board No. 648 sits on display next to the museum's Insley Building. No. 648 was brought to the United States from Australia in 1983 to take part in the Trolley Festival of San Francisco before being sold to the Western Railway Museum only a few years later.

From left to right: East Bay Street Railway No. 352, Key System No. 182, and Petaluma & Santa Rosa No. 63 sit on display awaiting their next call to service.

Key System 187 passes by a rural farm and the local wind farm on its way to Pantano.

Key System 187 leaves the Loring C. Jensen Memorial Car House to pick up passengers at the museum's main station platform.

Key System 1201 was originally built as a standard passenger coach to be pulled by steam locomotives for the California Railway in 1895. Later on in its career, it was motorized and converted to a line car by the Key System to maintain trolley wire until the Key System ended electric operation in 1958.

Right: The Key System Railway logo as seen from the side of line car 1201.

Below: East Bay Street Railway 352 making a station stop at Laflin Park.

Western Railway Museum maintenance of way equipment at Gum Grove.

Portland Traction Company 4001 eases its way through the yard back to the station.

Various pieces of interurban, streetcar, and electric railroad equipment sit on display inside of the Loring C. Jensen Memorial Car House.

Members and volunteers of the Western Railway Museum move equipment around the Loring C. Jensen Memorial Car House in preparation for the day ahead.

Melbourne & Metropolitan Tram Board No. 648 on outdoor display.

Another piece of maintenance of way equipment owned by the museum is seen here at Gum Grove.

Sacramento Northern 654 and caboose 1632 sit on outdoor display for public tours.

Sacramento Northern 654 eases out of the car house with its matching caboose in tow.

Petaluma & Santa Rosa interurban car No. 63 was built in 1904 by the Holman Car Company. From 1904 until its retirement in 1932, No. 63 ran passenger services between Petaluma, Sebastopol, Santa Rosa, and Forestville, California. It would then spend the next thirty-five years dismantled before becoming part of a house. The Bay Area Electric Railroad Association acquired No. 63 in 1967, and restoration was completed by 1973. Among the visiting public, No. 63 is one of the most popular pieces in the museum's collection.

Sacramento Northern 654 with matching caboose No. 1632.

San Diego Municipal Transit System 1018 and 1017 were built in 1981 for the San Diego, Arizona, and Eastern Railway between San Diego and San Ysidro. Donated to the Bay Area Electric Railroad association in 2014 by the SDMTS, these modern light rail vehicles helped revive America's interest in urban light rail transportation.

Key System 187 crossing Shiloh Road at Gum Grove.

Gum Grove is also the location of a small power station that helps generate electric power for the museum's main line to Birds Landing.

The museum maintains a wide variety of vintage electric railroad equipment that represents an era of railroading that has long since passed. By the end of World War II, the interurban railroads were either absorbed by other railroads of the time, became freight hauling shortline railroads, or simply went out of business.

San Francisco Municipal Railway 178 and 1003 sit quietly in their assigned car house on display.

Bibliography

"About Us," *Niles Canyon Railway: A Railroad Museum Where the Exhibits Come to Life*, ncry.org/about

"All Aboard the California State Railroad Museum's Excursion Railroad," *California State Railroad Museum*, californiarailroad.museum/visit/excursion-train-rides

"Niles Canyon Transcontinental Railroad Historic District," *National Park Service*, nps.gov/places/niles-canyon-transcontinental-railroad-historic-district.htm

"Saving Napa's Rail Line," *Napa Valley Wine Train*, winetrain.com/the-wine-train/saving-napas-rail-line

Hectman, Kevin H. *Sacramento Southern Railroad* (Arcadia Publishing, March 9, 2009), arcadiapublishing.com/9780738569864/Sacramento-Southern-Railroad

Western Railway Museum, wrm.org